AIR FRYER
COOKBOOK
FOR BEGINNERS

*Easy and Appetizing Recipes for Cooking with
the Air Method and Staying in Shape*

LUCAS BOOKS

Table of Contents

Sommario

—

5

Introduction

What is an Air Fryer

The air fryer is an amped-up countertop convection oven. the small appliance claims to mimic the results of deep-frying with nothing quite hot air and tiny or no oil.

This gadget has surged in popularity over a previous couple of years. There are all types of belongings you can air-fry—from frozen chicken wings and homemade french-fried potatoes to roasted vegetables and fresh-baked cookies.

How Do Air Fryers Work?

The top section of an air fryer holds a heating mechanism and fan. You place the food during a fryer-style basket and once you turn it on, hot air rushes down and round the food. This rapid circulation makes the food crisp—much like deep-frying, but without the oil.

Here's the way to use an air fryer:

1. Place your food within the basket
Depending on your air fryer's size, the basket may hold anywhere from 2 to 10 quarts. In most cases, you'll want to feature 1 or 2 teaspoons of oil to assist the food get nice and crispy.

2. Set the time and temperature
Air fryer cooking times and temperatures typically range from 5 to 25 minutes at 350° to 400°F, counting on the food you're cooking.

3. Let the food cook
In some cases, you'll get to flip or turn the food halfway through the cooking time to assist it to crisp up evenly. Once you're done cooking, it's important to wash your air fryer.

What are you able to Cook in an Air Fryer?

While many of the simplest air-fryer recipes are foods that are typically deep-fried, you'll also use this appliance to roast vegetables, cook meat, and bake cookies.

Frozen Finger Foods
The air fryer may be a star when it involves preparing frozen foods that are meant to taste deep-fried. Frozen french-fried potatoes, mozzarella sticks, and chicken nuggets are a number of the various frozen air-fried foods you'll make.

Homemade Finger Foods
If you favor forming your finger foods from scratch, the air fryer may be a great option for creating crispy homemade snacks and sides—try Air-Fryer Sweet Potato Fries, Air-Fryer Pickles, or Air-Fryer Papas Rellenas.

Chicken, Fish, and Meat
Air fryers aren't only for greasy carbs—you also can make dishes that are full of protein. Try air-fryer chicken recipes, like Air-Fryer Nashville Hot Chicken. For a healthier option, Air-Fryer Keto Meatballs are an excellent choice. When it involves fish and seafood dishes, we love this Air-Fryer Crumb-Topped Sole.

Roasted Vegetables
Since air fryers are essentially small convection ovens, they're great for roasting vegetables—especially if you're only cooking for one or two people. a number of our favorite air-fryer vegetable recipes include Air-Fryer Herb and Lemon Cauliflower and Air-Fryer Garlic-Rosemary Brussels Sprouts.

However, when you're using this gadget to cook veggies, skip the leafy greens.

Some food
Air fryers are often great for creating single-serving desserts, including small food like cookies and apple fritters (here's the way to make air-fryer cookies). you'll also try making these Air-Fryer Peppermint Lava

Cakes for the winter holidays or these Air-Fryer Mini Nutella Doughnut Holes for an indulgent treat any time of year.

However, you can't make anything that uses a liquid batter (unless you freeze it first).

Air Fryer Tips

Is air-fried food healthy?
You could argue that air-fried food is healthier than deep-fried food because it uses less oil. Frozen french-fried potatoes prepared within the air fryer contain between 4 and 6 grams of fat versus their deep-fried counterparts, which have a whopping 17 grams per serving.

Air fryers make it easy to whomp up frozen foods, and that they can do so in a way that's healthier than deep-frying. The results are far better than oven-frying, and your kitchen stays cool.

Even the most important air fryers have a limited capacity, so you'll likely need to cook in batches—especially if you're preparing food for a crowd. Bigger than a toaster, air fryers also take up valuable counter space. Finally, they will be pricey, counting on the model you get.

With numerous models on the market, this popular appliance has come down in price within a previous couple of years—many models cost but $200 and a few cost but $100.

In any case, the advantages of owning an air fryer are many because of the numerous recipes you can prepare and some of them are contained in this cookbook.

Enjoy your meal and have fun!

LUCAS BOOKS

Chicken

Turkey Sausage Breakfast Cups

Ingredients

1 smoked turkey sausage, chopped
4 eggs
4 tablespoons cream cheese
4 tablespoons cheddar cheese, shredded
4 tablespoons fresh scallions, chopped
1/2 teaspoon garlic, minced
1/4 teaspoon mustard seeds
1/4 teaspoon chili powder
Salt and red pepper, to taste

Directions

Divide the chopped sausage between four silicone baking cups.
In a mixing bowl, beat the eggs until pale and frothy. Then, add in the remaining ingredients and mix to combine well.
Pour the egg mixture into the cups.
Cook in your Air Fryer at 330 degrees F for 10 to 11 minutes.
Transfer the cups to wire racks to cool slightly before unmolding.

Per serving: 619 Calories; 48.2g Fat; 5.9g Carbs; 37.2g Protein; 2.6g Sugars

Keto Chicken Quesadillas

(Ready in about 25 minutes | Servings 2)

Ingredients

1/2 pound chicken breasts, boneless and skinless
Salt to taste
3 eggs
4 ounces Ricotta cheese
2 tablespoons flaxseed meal
1 teaspoon psyllium husk powder
Black pepper, to taste

Directions

Cook the chicken in the preheated Air Fryer at 380 degrees F for 12 minutes; turn the chicken over halfway through the cooking time.
Salt to taste and slice into small strips.
In a mixing bowl, beat the eggs, cheese, flaxseed meal, psyllium husk powder and black pepper. Spoon the mixture into a lightly oiled baking pan.
Bake at 380 degrees F for 9 to 10 minutes.
Spoon the chicken pieces onto your quesadilla and fold in half. Cut your quesadilla into two pieces and serve.

Per serving: 401 Calories; 20.5g Fat; 5.7g Carbs; 48.3g Protein; 0.6g Sugars

Chinese-Style Turkey Thighs

(Ready in about 35 minutes | Servings 6)

Ingredient

1 tablespoon sesame oil
2 pounds turkey thighs
1 teaspoon Chinese Five-spice powder
1 teaspoon pink Himalayan salt
1/4 teaspoon Sichuan pepper
6 tablespoons honey
1 tablespoon Chinese rice vinegar
2 tablespoons soy sauce
1 tablespoon sweet chili sauce
1 tablespoon mustard

Directions

Preheat your Air Fryer to 360 degrees F.
Brush the sesame oil all over the turkey thighs. Season them with spices.
Cook for 23 minutes, turning over once or twice. Make sure to work in batches to ensure even cooking
In the meantime, combine the remaining ingredients in a wok (or similar type pan) that is preheated over medium-high heat. Cook and stir until the sauce reduces by about a third.
Add the fried turkey thighs to the wok; gently stir to coat with the sauce.

Per serving: 279 Calories; 10.1g Fat; 19g Carbs; 27.7g Protein; 17.9g Sugars

Turkey Tenderloins with Baby Potatoes

(Ready in about 50 minutes | Servings 6)

Ingredients

2 pounds turkey tenderloins
2 teaspoons olive oil
Salt and ground black pepper, to taste
1 teaspoon smoked paprika
2 tablespoons dry white wine
1 tablespoon fresh tarragon leaves, chopped
1 pound baby potatoes, rubbed

Directions

Brush the turkey tenderloins with olive oil. Season with salt, black pepper, and paprika.
Afterwards, add the white wine and tarragon.
Cook the turkey tenderloins at 350 degrees F for 30 minutes, flipping them over halfway through. Let them rest for 5 to 9 minutes before slicing and serving.
After that, spritz the sides and bottom of the cooking basket with the remaining 1 teaspoon of olive oil.
Then, preheat your Air Fryer to 400 degrees F; cook the baby potatoes for 15 minutes. Serve with the turkey.

Per serving: 317 Calories; 7.4g Fat; 14.2g Carbs; 45.7g Protein; 1.1g Sugars

Greek-Style Chicken Salad

(Ready in about 20 minutes | Servings 2)

19

Ingredients
1/2 pound chicken breasts, boneless and skinless
1 cup grape tomatoes, halved
1 Serrano pepper, deveined and chopped
2 bell peppers, deveined and chopped
2 tablespoons olives, pitted and sliced
1 cucumber, sliced
1 red onion, sliced
1 cup arugula
1 cup baby spinach
1/4 cup mayonnaise
2 tablespoons Greek-style yogurt
1 teaspoon lime juice
1/4 teaspoon oregano
1/4 teaspoon basil
1/4 teaspoon red pepper flakes, crushed
Sea salt and ground black pepper, to taste

Directions
Spritz the chicken breasts with a nonstick cooking oil.

Cook in the preheated Air Fryer at 380 degrees F for 12 minutes.

Transfer to a cutting board to cool slightly before slicing.

Cut the chicken into bite-sized strips and transfer them to a salad bowl.

Toss the chicken with the remaining ingredients and place in your refrigerator until ready to serve.

Per serving: 391 Calories; 21.3g Fat; 24g Carbs; 28.4g Protein; 16g Sugars

Pork

Fried Bacon

(Ready in about 10 minutes | Servings 4)

Ingredients

1/2 pound bacon slices
1/2 cup tomato ketchup
1/4 teaspoon cayenne pepper
1/4 teaspoon dried marjoram
1 teaspoon Sriracha sauce

Directions

Place the bacon slices in the cooking basket.
Cook the bacon slices at 400 degrees F for about 8 minutes.
Meanwhile, make the sauce by mixing the remaining ingredients.
Serve the warm bacon with the sauce on the side.

Per serving: 235 Calories; 23g Fat; 1.3g Carbs; 7.3g Protein; 1.1g Sugars

BBQ-Glazed Meatloaf Muffins

(Ready in about 45 minutes | Servings 3)

Ingredients

1 pound lean ground pork
1 small onion, chopped
2 cloves garlic, crushed
1/4 cup carrots, grated
1 serrano pepper, seeded and minced
1 teaspoon stone-ground mustard
1/4 cup crackers, crushed
1 egg, lightly beaten
Sea salt and ground black pepper, to taste
1/2 cup BBQ sauce

Directions

Mix all ingredients, except for the BBQ sauce, until everything is well incorporated.

Brush a muffin tin with vegetable oil. Use an ice cream scoop to spoon the meat mixture into the cups. Top each meatloaf cup with a spoonful of BBQ sauce.

Bake in the preheated Air Fryer at 395 degrees F for about 40 minutes. Transfer to a cooling rack.

Wait for a few minutes before unmolding and serving.

Per serving: 269 Calories; 9.7g Fat; 9.1g Carbs; 36.6g Protein; 4.4g Sugars

BBQ Ribs

(Ready in about 40 minutes | Servings 2)

Ingredients

1/2 pound ribs
Sea salt and black pepper, to taste
1/2 teaspoon red chili flakes
1 tablespoon agave syrup
1/2 teaspoon garlic powder
1/2 cup tomato paste
1 teaspoon brown mustard
1 tablespoon balsamic vinegar
1 tablespoon Worcestershire sauce

Directions

Place the pork ribs, salt, black pepper and red pepper flakes in a Ziplock bag; shake until the ribs are coated on all sides.
Roast in the preheated Air Fryer at 350 degrees F for 35 minutes.
In a saucepan over medium heat, heat all sauce ingredients, bringing to a boil. Turn the heat to a simmer until the sauce has reduced by half.
Spoon the sauce over the ribs and serve warm.

Per serving:492 Calories; 33.5g Fat; 26.8g Carbs; 22.5g Protein; 19.7g Sugars

Pork with Padrón Peppers

(Ready in about 30 minutes | Servings 4)

Ingredients

1 tablespoon olive oil

8 ounces Padrón peppers

2 pounds pork loin, sliced

1 teaspoon Celtic salt

1 teaspoon paprika

1 heaped tablespoon capers, drained

8 green olives, pitted and halved

Directions

Drizzle olive oil all over the Padrón peppers; cook them in the preheated Air Fryer at 400 degrees F for 10 minutes, turning occasionally, until well blistered all over and tender-crisp.

Then, turn the temperature to 360 degrees F.

Season the pork loin with salt and paprika. Add the capers and cook for 16 minutes, turning them over halfway through the cooking time.

Serve with olives and the reserved Padrón peppers.

Per serving: 536 Calories; 29.5g Fat; 5.9g Carbs; 59g Protein; 2.9g Sugars

Pork Loin with Mushroom Sauce

(Ready in about 30 minutes | Servings 4)

Ingredients

1 pounds top loin, boneless

1 tablespoon olive oil

1 teaspoon Celtic salt

1/4 teaspoon ground black pepper, or more to taste

2 shallots, sliced

2 garlic cloves, minced

1 cup mushrooms, chopped

2 tablespoons all-purpose flour

3/4 cup cream of mushroom soup

1 teaspoon chili powder

Salt, to taste

Directions

Pat dry the pork and drizzle with olive oil. Season with Celtic salt and pepper. Cook in the preheated Air Fryer at 370 degrees F for 10 minutes.

Top with shallot slices and cook another 10 minutes.

Test the temperature of the meat; it should be around 150 degrees F. Reserve the pork and onion, keeping warm.

Add the cooking juices to a saucepan and preheat over medium-high heat. Cook the garlic and mushrooms until aromatic about 2 minutes.

Combine the flour with the mushroom soup. Add the flour mixture to the pan along with the chili powder and salt. Gradually stir into the pan.

Bring to a boil; immediately turn the heat to medium and cook for 2 to 3 minutes stirring frequently. Spoon the sauce over the reserved pork and onion.

Per serving: 416 Calories; 13.9g Fat; 15.2g Carbs; 55.1g Protein; 4.4g Sugars

---

Beef

Chuck Roast with Potatoes

(Ready in about 50 minutes | Servings 3)

Ingredients

1 tablespoon brown mustard
2 tablespoons tomato paste, preferably homemade
2 tablespoons BBQ sauce
1 tablespoon Worcester sauce
1 ½ pounds chuck roast
1 pound medium-sized russet potatoes, quartered
Coarse sea salt and ground black pepper, to taste
1/2 teaspoon cayenne pepper
1 teaspoon shallot powder
1 teaspoon granulated garlic
1 teaspoon dried marjoram

Directions

Mix the mustard, tomato paste, BBQ sauce and Worcester sauce in a small bowl. Rub this mixture all over the chuck roast.
Add spices and place the chuck roast in the Air Fryer cooking basket that is lightly greased with melted butter.
Air fry at 400 degrees F for 30 minutes; turn it over and scatter potato chunks around the beef. Continue to cook an additional 15 minutes. Double check to make sure the beef is cooked thoroughly. Taste and adjust seasonings. Place the meat on a cutting board. Slice the beef against the grain and eat warm.

Per serving: 438 Calories; 13.1g Fat; 30.8g Carbs; 50g Protein; 2.9g Sugars

Roast Beef with Vegetables

(Ready in about 45 minutes + marinating time | Servings 3)

Ingredients

1 pound beef roast
1 teaspoon brown mustard
1/4 cup apple juice
1 tablespoon fish sauce
1 tablespoon honey
1/2 teaspoon dried dill
1/2 teaspoon dried thyme
2 medium-sized carrots, sliced
1 parsnip, sliced
1 red onion, sliced
Sea salt and ground black pepper, to taste
1 teaspoon paprika

Directions

Toss the beef roast with the mustard, apple juice, fish sauce, honey, dill and thyme in a glass bowl. Cover and let it marinate in your refrigerator overnight.

Add the marinated beef roast to the cooking basket, discarding the marinade.

Roast in your Air Fryer at 400 degrees F for 40 minutes. Turn the beef over and baste with the reserved marinade.

Add the carrots, parsnip and onion to the cooking basket; continue to cook for 12 minutes more.

Season the beef and vegetables with salt, black pepper and paprika. Serve warm.

Per serving: 272 Calories; 8.9g Fat; 17.1g Carbs; 32.1g Protein; 10.3g Sugars

Hungarian Oven Stew

(Ready in about 1 hour 10 minutes | Servings 4)

Ingredients

4 tablespoons all-purpose flour
Sea salt and cracked black pepper, to taste
1 teaspoon Hungarian paprika
1 pound beef chuck roast, boneless, cut into bite-sized cubes
2 teaspoons sunflower oil
1 medium-sized leek, chopped
2 garlic cloves, minced
2 bay leaves
1 teaspoon caraway seeds.
2 cups roasted vegetable broth
2 ripe tomatoes, pureed
2 tablespoons red wine
2 bell peppers, chopped
2 medium carrots, sliced
1 celery stalk, peeled and diced

Directions

Add the flour, salt, black pepper, paprika, and beef to a resealable bag; shake to coat well.
Heat the oil in a Dutch oven over medium-high flame; sauté the leeks, garlic, bay leaves, and caraway seeds about 4 minutes or until fragrant. Transfer to a lightly greased baking pan.
Then, brown the beef, stirring occasionally, working in batches. Add to the baking pan.
Add the vegetable broth, tomatoes, and red wine. Lower the pan onto the Air Fryer basket. Bake at 325 degrees F for 40 minutes. Add the bell peppers, carrots, and celery. Cook an additional 20 minutes. Serve immediately.

Per serving:375 Calories; 16.1g Fat; 16.5g Carbs; 39.6g Protein; 4.6g Sugars

Beef with Peanut Sauce

(Ready in about 25 minutes + marinating time | Servings 4)

Ingredients

2 pounds filet mignon, sliced into bite-sized strips
1 tablespoon oyster sauce
2 tablespoons sesame oil
2 tablespoons tamari sauce
1 tablespoon ginger-garlic paste
1 tablespoon mustard
1 tablespoon honey
1 teaspoon chili powder
1/4 cup peanut butter
2 tablespoons lime juice
1 teaspoon red pepper flakes
2 tablespoons water

Directions

Place the beef strips, oyster sauce, sesame oil, tamari sauce, ginger-garlic paste, mustard, honey, and chili powder in a large ceramic dish.
Cover and allow it to marinate for 2 hours in your refrigerator.
Cook in the preheated Air Fryer at 400 degrees F for 18 minutes, shaking the basket occasionally.
Mix the peanut butter with lime juice, red pepper flakes, and water.
Spoon the sauce onto the air fried beef strips and serve warm.

Per serving: 425 Calories; 20.1g Fat; 11.2g Carbs; 50g Protein; 7.9g Sugars

Indian Beef Samosas

(Ready in about 35 minutes | Servings 8)

Ingredients

1 tablespoon sesame oil

4 tablespoons shallots, minced

2 cloves garlic, minced

2 tablespoons green chili peppers, chopped

1/2 pound ground chuck

4 ounces bacon, chopped

Salt and ground black pepper, to taste

1 teaspoon cumin powder

1 teaspoon turmeric

1 teaspoon coriander

1 cup frozen peas, thawed

1 (16-ounce) package phyllo dough

1 egg, beaten with 2 tablespoons of water (egg wash)

Directions

Heat the oil in a saucepan over medium-high heat. Once hot, sauté the shallots, garlic, and chili peppers until tender, about 3 minutes. Then, add the beef and bacon; continue to sauté an additional 4 minutes, crumbling with a fork. Season with the salt, pepper, cumin powder, turmeric, and coriander. Stir in peas.

Then, preheat your Air Fryer to 330 degrees F. Brush the Air Fryer basket with cooking oil.

Place 1 to 2 tablespoons of the mixture onto each phyllo sheet. Fold the sheets into triangles, pressing the edges. Brush the tops with egg wash.

Bake for 7 to 8 minutes, working with batches. Serve with Indian tomato sauce if desired.

Per serving. 266 Calories; 13g Fat; 24.5g Carbs; 12.2g Protein; 1.5g Sugars

Fish

Pancetta-Wrapped Scallops

(Ready in about 10 minutes | Servings 3)

Ingredients

1 pound sea scallops

1 tablespoon deli mustard

2 tablespoons soy sauce

1/4 teaspoon shallot powder

1/4 teaspoon garlic powder

1/2 teaspoon dried dill

Sea salt and ground black pepper, to taste

4 ounces pancetta slices

Directions

Pat dry the sea scallops and transfer them to a mixing bowl. Toss the sea scallops with the deli mustard, soy sauce, shallot powder, garlic powder, dill, salt and black pepper.

Wrap a slice of bacon around each scallop and transfer them to the Air Fryer cooking basket.

Cook in your Air Fryer at 400 degrees F for 4 minutes; turn them over and cook an additional 3 minutes.

Serve with hot sauce for dipping if desired.

Per serving: 403 Calories; 24.5g Fat; 5.1g Carbs; 40.1g Protein; 3.1g Sugars

Cod Fillets

(Ready in about 15 minutes | Servings 2)

Ingredients

1 cod fish fillets

1 teaspoon butter, melted

1 teaspoon Old Bay seasoning

1 egg, beaten

2 tablespoons coconut milk, unsweetened

1/3 cup coconut flour, unsweetened

Directions

Place the cod fish fillets, butter and Old Bay seasoning in a Ziplock bag; shake until the fish is well coated on all sides.

In a shallow bowl, whisk the egg and coconut milk until frothy.

In another bowl, place the coconut flour. Dip the fish fillets in the egg mixture, then, coat them with coconut flour, pressing to adhere. Cook the fish at 390 degrees F for 6 minutes; flip them over and cook an additional 6 minutes until your fish flakes easily when tested with a fork.

Per serving: 218 Calories; 12.5g Fat; 3.5g Carbs; 22g Protein; 1.9g Sugars

Crispy Mustardy Fish Fingers

(Ready in about 20 minutes | Servings 4)

Ingredients

1 ½ pounds tilapia pieces (fingers)
1/2 cup all-purpose flour
2 eggs
1 tablespoon yellow mustard
1 cup cornmeal
1 teaspoon garlic powder
1 teaspoon onion powder
Sea salt and ground black pepper, to taste
1/2 teaspoon celery powder
2 tablespoons peanut oil

Directions

Pat dry the fish fingers with a kitchen towel.
To make a breading station, place the all-purpose flour in a shallow
dish. In a separate dish, whisk the eggs with mustard.
In a third bowl, mix the remaining ingredients.
Dredge the fish fingers in the flour, shaking the excess into the bowl;
dip in the egg mixture and turn to coat evenly; then, dredge in the
cornmeal mixture, turning a couple of times to coat evenly.
Cook in the preheated Air Fryer at 390 degrees F for 5 minutes; turn
them over and cook another 5 minutes.

**Per serving: 468 Calories; 12.7g Fat; 45.6g Carbs; 41.9g Protein;
1.4g Sugars**

Salmon Patties

(Ready in about 15 minutes | Servings 4)

Ingredients

1 pound salmon

1 egg

1 garlic clove, minced

2 green onions, minced

1/2 cup rolled oats Sauce:

1 teaspoon rice wine

1 ½ tablespoons soy sauce

1 teaspoon honey

A pinch of salt

1 teaspoon gochugaru (Korean red chili pepper flakes)

Directions

Start by preheating your Air Fryer to 380 degrees F. Spritz the Air Fryer basket with cooking oil.

Mix the salmon, egg, garlic, green onions, and rolled oats in a bowl; knead with your hands until everything is well incorporated.

Shape the mixture into equally sized patties. Transfer your patties to the Air Fryer basket.

Cook the fish patties for 10 minutes, turning them over halfway through.

Meanwhile, make the sauce by whisking all ingredients. Serve the warm fish patties with the sauce on the side.

Per serving: 396 Calories; 20.1g Fat; 16.7g Carbs; 35.2g Protein; 3.1g Sugars

Shrimp Scampi Linguine

(Ready in about 25 minutes | Servings 4)

Ingredients

1 ½ pounds shrimp, shelled and deveined

1/2 tablespoon fresh basil leaves, chopped

2 tablespoons olive oil

2 cloves garlic, minced

1/2 teaspoon fresh ginger, grated

1/4 teaspoon cracked black pepper

1/2 teaspoon sea salt

1/4 cup chicken stock

2 ripe tomatoes, pureed

8 ounces linguine pasta

1/2 cup parmesan cheese, preferably freshly grated

Directions

Start by preheating the Air Fryer to 395 degrees F. Place the shrimp, basil, olive oil, garlic, ginger, black pepper, salt, chicken stock, and tomatoes in the casserole dish.

Transfer the casserole dish to the cooking basket and bake for 10 minutes.

Bring a large pot of lightly salted water to a boil. Cook the linguine for 10 minutes or until al dente; drain.

Divide between four serving plates. Add the shrimp sauce and top with parmesan cheese.

Per serving: 560 Calories; 15.1g Fat; 47.3g Carbs; 59.3g Protein; 1.6g Sugars

Vegetable and Side Dishes

Stuffed and Baked Potatoes

(Ready in about 35 minutes | Servings 2)

Ingredients

2 medium sweet potatoes
6 ounces canned kidney beans
1/4 cup Cotija cheese, crumbled
1 tablespoon butter, cold
Coarse sea salt and ground black pepper, to taste
2 tablespoons cilantro, chopped

Directions

Poke the sweet potatoes all over using a small knife; transfer them to the Air Fryer cooking basket.
Cook in the preheated Air Fryer at 380 degrees F for 20 to 25 minutes. Then, scrape the sweet potato flesh using a spoon; mix sweet potato flesh with kidney beans, cheese, butter, salt and pepper.
Bake for a further 10 minutes until cooked through.
Place the sweet potatoes on serving plates. Garnish with cilantro and serve.

Per serving: 277 Calories; 13.7g Fat; 31.4g Carbs; 8.1g Protein; 9.9g Sugars

Cauliflower Tater Tots

(Ready in about 20 minutes | Servings 3)

Ingredients

1 ½ pounds cauliflower

1 tablespoon butter

2 tablespoons plain flour

1 tablespoon corn flour

1 teaspoon shallot powder

1/2 teaspoon garlic powder

1 teaspoon dried parsley flakes

1/2 teaspoon dried basil

Sea salt and freshly ground black pepper, to taste

Directions

Blanch the cauliflower in salted boiling water until al dente about 4 minutes. Drain your cauliflower well and pulse in a food processor. Transfer the cauliflower to a mixing bowl. Stir in the remaining ingredients and mix to combine well. Roll the mixture into bite-sized tots.

Cook in the preheated Air Fryer at 375 degrees F for 16 minutes, shaking the basket halfway through the cooking time to ensure even browning.

Per serving: 127 Calories; 4.6g Fat; 17.6g Carbs; 5.2g Protein; 4.4g Sugars

Crispy Wax Beans with Almonds and Blue Cheese

(Ready in about 15 minutes | Servings 3)

Ingredients

1 pound wax beans, cleaned

2 tablespoons peanut oil

4 tablespoons seasoned breadcrumbs

Sea salt and ground black pepper, to taste

1/2 teaspoon red pepper flakes, crushed

2 tablespoons almonds, sliced

1/3 cup blue cheese, crumbled

Directions

Toss the wax beans with the peanut oil, breadcrumbs, salt, black pepper, and red pepper.

Place the wax beans in the lightly greased cooking basket.

Cook in the preheated Air Fryer at 400 degrees F for 5 minutes. Shake the basket once or twice.

Add the almonds and cook for 3 minutes more or until lightly toasted. Serve topped with blue cheese.

Per serving: 242 Calories; 16.9g Fat; 16.3g Carbs; 6.8g Protein; 3.5g Sugars

Cheese Stuffed Roasted Peppers

(Ready in about 20 minutes | Servings 2)

Ingredients

2 red bell peppers, tops and seeds removed
2 yellow bell peppers, tops and seeds removed
Salt and pepper, to taste
1 cup cream cheese
4 tablespoons mayonnaise
2 pickles, chopped

Directions

Arrange the peppers in the lightly greased cooking basket. Cook in the preheated Air Fryer at 400 degrees F for 15 minutes, turning them over halfway through the cooking time.
Season with salt and pepper.
Then, in a mixing bowl, combine the cream cheese with the mayonnaise and chopped pickles.
Stuff the pepper with the cream cheese mixture and serve.

Per serving: 367 Calories; 21.8g Fat; 21.9g Carbs; 21.5g Protein; 14.1g Sugars

Winter Bliss Bowl

(Ready in about 45 minutes | Servings 3)

Ingredients

1 cup pearled barley
1 (1-pound) head cauliflower, broken into small florets
Coarse sea salt and ground black pepper, to taste
2 tablespoons champagne vinegar
4 tablespoons mayonnaise
1 teaspoon yellow mustard
4 tablespoons olive oil, divided
10 ounces ounce canned sweet corn, drained
2 tablespoons cilantro leaves, chopped

Directions

Cook the barley in a saucepan with salted water. Bring to a boil and cook approximately 28 minutes. Drain and reserve.
Start by preheating the Air Fryer to 400 degrees F.
Place the cauliflower florets in the lightly greased Air Fryer basket. Season with salt and black pepper; cook for 12 minutes, tossing halfway through the cooking time.
Toss with the reserved barley. Add the champagne vinegar, mayonnaise, mustard, olive oil, and corn. Garnish with fresh cilantro.

Per serving: 387 Calories; 25.3g Fat; 38.5g Carbs; 6g Protein; 5.8g Sugars

SNACKS & APPETIZERS

Avocado Fries with Lime

(Ready in about 15 minutes | Servings 4)

Ingredients

1/2 cup plain flour
1/2 milk
1/2 cup tortilla chips, crushed
1/2 teaspoon red pepper flakes, crushed
Sea salt and ground black pepper, to taste
2 avocados, peeled, pitted and sliced
1/2 cup Greek yogurt
4 tablespoons mayonnaise
1 teaspoon fresh lime juice
1/2 teaspoon lime chili seasoning salt

Directions

Mix the plain flour and milk in a plate.
Add the crushed tortilla chips, red pepper flakes, salt and black pepper to another rimmed plate. Dredge the avocado slices in the flour mixture and then, coat them in the crushed tortilla chips.
Cook the avocado at 390 degrees F for about 8 minutes, shaking the basket halfway through the cooking time.
In the meantime, mix the remaining ingredients, until well combined.
Serve warm avocado fries with the lime sauce.

Per serving: 371 Calories; 27.5g Fat; 27.1g Carbs; 6.4g Protein; 4.5g Suga

Prosciutto Stuffed Jalapeños

(Ready in about 15 minutes | Servings 2)

Ingredients

8 fresh jalapeño peppers, deseeded and cut in half lengthwise
4 ounces Ricotta cheese, at room temperature
1/4 teaspoon cayenne pepper
1/2 teaspoon granulated garlic
8 slices prosciutto, chopped

Directions

Place the fresh jalapeño peppers on a clean surface.
Mix the remaining ingredients in a bowl; divide the filling between the jalapeño peppers. Transfer the peppers to the Air Fryer cooking basket.
Cook the stuffed peppers at 400 degrees F for 15 minutes. Serve.

Per serving: 178 Calories; 8.7g Fat; 11.7g Carbs; 14.3g Protein; 4.6g Sugars

Cajun Cheese Sticks

(Ready in about 15 minutes | Servings 4)

Ingredients

1/2 cup all-purpose flour
2 eggs
1/2 cup parmesan cheese, grated
1 tablespoon Cajun seasonings
8 cheese sticks, kid-friendly
1/4 cup ketchup

Directions

To begin, set up your breading station. Place the all-purpose flour in a shallow dish. In a separate dish, whisk the eggs.
Finally, mix the parmesan cheese and Cajun seasoning in a third dish. Start by dredging the cheese sticks in the flour; then, dip them into the egg. Press the cheese sticks into the parmesan mixture, coating evenly.
Place the breaded cheese sticks in the lightly greased Air Fryer basket. Cook at 380 degrees F for 6 minutes.
Serve with ketchup.

Per serving: 372 Calories; 22.7g Fat; 19.5g Carbs; 21.8g Protein; 3.8g Sugars

Cheese and Broccoli Balls

(Ready in about 25 minutes | Servings 4)

Ingredients

1/2 pound broccoli
1/2 cup Romano cheese, grated
1 garlic cloves, minced
1 shallot, chopped
4 eggs, beaten
2 tablespoons butter, at room temperature
1/2 teaspoon paprika
1/4 teaspoon dried basil
Sea salt and ground black pepper, to taste

Directions

Add the broccoli to your food processor and pulse until the consistency resembles rice.
Stir in the remaining ingredients; mix until everything is well combined. Shape the mixture into bite-sized balls and transfer them to the lightly greased cooking basket.
Cook in the preheated Air Fryer at 375 degrees F for 16 minutes, shaking halfway through the cooking time. Serve with cocktail sticks and tomato ketchup on the side

Per serving: 192 Calories; 15.2g Fat; 2.9g Carbs; 11.5g Protein; 0.6g Sugars

.

Chicken Nuggets with Spicy Sauce

(Ready in about 20 minutes | Servings 6)

Ingredients

1 pound chicken breasts, slice into tenders
1/2 teaspoon cayenne pepper
Salt and black pepper, to taste
1/4 cup cornmeal
1 egg, whisked
1/2 cup seasoned breadcrumbs
1/4 cup mayo
1/4 cup barbecue sauce

Directions

Pat the chicken tenders dry with a kitchen towel. Season with the cayenne pepper, salt, and black pepper.

Dip the chicken tenders into the cornmeal, followed by the egg.

Press the chicken tenders into the breadcrumbs, coating evenly.

Place the chicken tenders in the lightly greased Air Fryer basket.

Cook at 360 degrees for 9 to 12 minutes, turning them over to cook evenly.

In a mixing bowl, thoroughly combine the mayonnaise with the barbecue sauce. Serve the chicken nuggets with the sauce for dipping.

Per serving: 211 Calories; 5.4g Fat; 18.4g Carbs; 18.9g Protein; 6.3g Sugars

Rice and Grains

Pizza Margherita

(Ready in about 15 minutes | Servings 1)

Ingredients

6-inch dough
2 tablespoons tomato sauce
2 ounces mozzarella
1 teaspoon extra-virgin olive oil
Coarse sea salt, to taste
2-3 fresh basil leaves

Directions

Start by preheating your Air Fryer to 380 degrees F.
Stretch the dough on a pizza peel lightly dusted with flour. Spread with a layer of tomato sauce.
Add mozzarella to the crust and drizzle with olive oil. Salt to taste.
Bake in the preheated Air Fryer for 4 minutes. Rotate the baking tray and bake for a further 4 minutes. Garnish with fresh basil leaves and serve immediately.

Per serving: 531 Calories; 24.1g Fat; 57.7g Carbs; 20.9g Protein; 7.1g Sugars

Honey Cornbread Muffins

(Ready in about 20 minutes | Servings 3)

Ingredients

1/2 cup cornmeal
1/2 cup plain flour
1 tablespoon flaxseed meal
1 teaspoon baking powder
3 tablespoons honey
A pinch of coarse sea salt
A pinch of grated nutmeg
1/2 teaspoon ground cinnamon
1 egg, whisked
3/4 cup milk
2 tablespoons butter, melted

Directions

In a mixing bowl, thoroughly combine the dry ingredients. In another bowl, mix the wet ingredients.
Then, stir the wet mixture into the dry mixture.
Pour the batter into a lightly buttered muffin tin. Now, bake your cornbread muffins at 350 degrees F for about 20 minutes.
Check for doneness with a toothpick and transfer to a wire rack to cool slightly before serving.

Per serving. 382 Calories; 13.1g Fat; 53g Carbs; 8.5g Protein; 20.9g Sugars

Buckwheat and Potato Flat Bread

(Ready in about 20 minutes | Servings 4)

Ingredients

4 potatoes, medium-sized
1 cup buckwheat flour
1/2 teaspoon salt
1/2 teaspoon red chili powder
1/4 cup honey

Directions

Put the potatoes into a large saucepan; add water to cover by about 1 inch. Bring to a boil. Then, lower the heat, and let your potatoes simmer about 8 minutes until they are fork tender.
Mash the potatoes and add the flour, salt, and chili powder. Create 4 balls and flatten them with a rolling pin
Bake in the preheated Air Fryer at 390 degrees F for 6 minutes.
Serve warm with honey.

Per serving: 334 Calories; 1.2g Fat; 77.3g Carbs; 8.4g Protein; 19.5g Sugars

Spinach Cheese Pie

(Ready in about 30 minutes | Servings 4)

Ingredients

1 (16-ounce) refrigerated rolled pie crusts
4 eggs, beaten
1/2 cup buttermilk
1/2 teaspoon salt
1/2 teaspoon garlic powder
1/4 teaspoon cayenne pepper
2 cups spinach, torn into pieces
1 cup Swiss cheese, shredded
2 tablespoons scallions, chopped

Directions

Unroll the pie crust and press it into a cake pan, crimping the top
edges if desired.
In a mixing dish, whisk together the eggs, buttermilk, salt, garlic,
powder, and cayenne pepper.
Add the spinach, 1/2 of Swiss cheese, and scallions into the pie
crust; pour the egg mixture over the top. Sprinkle the remaining 1/2
cup of Swiss cheese on top of the egg mixture.
Bake in the preheated Air Fryer at 350 degrees F for 10 minutes.
Rotate the cake pan and bake an additional 10 minutes.
Transfer to a wire rack to cool for 5 to 10 minutes. Serve warm.

**Per serving: 521 Calories; 33.9g Fat; 36.1g Carbs; 17.9g Protein;
5.2g Sugars**

Grilled Avocado Toast

(Ready in about 15 minutes | Servings 2)

Ingredients

4 slices artisan bread

1 garlic clove, halved

2 tablespoons olive oil

1 avocado, seeded, peeled and mashed

1/2 teaspoon sea salt

1/4 teaspoon ground black pepper

Directions

Rub 1 side of each bread slice with garlic. Brush with olive oil.
Place the bread slices on the Air Fryer grill pan. Bake in the
preheated Air Fryer at 400 degrees F for 3 to 4 minutes.
Slather the mashed avocado on top of the toast and season with salt
and pepper.

**Per serving: 389 Calories; 29.5g Fat; 28.8g Carbs; 5.6g Protein;
2.9g Sugars**

Vegan

Cajun Celery Sticks

(Ready in about 20 minutes | Servings 3)

Ingredients

1/2 pound celery root, peeled and cut into 1/2-inch sticks
1 teaspoon Cajun seasoning mix
Salt and white pepper, to taste
Sauce:
1/3 cup tofu mayonnaise
1 teaspoon lime juice
1 teaspoon deli mustard
1 teaspoon agave nectar

Directions

Toss the celery sticks with the Cajun seasoning mix, salt and white pepper and place them in the Air Fryer cooking basket.
Now, cook the celery sticks at 400 degrees F for about 17 minutes, shaking the basket halfway through the cooking time.
In the meantime, mix the mayonnaise with the lime juice, deli mustard and agave nectar.
Serve the celery sticks with the mayo sauce on the side.

Per serving: 108 Calories; 8.6g Fat; 5.2g Carbs; 2.4g Protein; 2.4g Sugars

Buffalo Cauliflower Bites

(Ready in about 35 minutes | Servings 2)

Ingredients

1/2 pound cauliflower florets
1/2 cup all-purpose flour
1/2 cup rice milk
1/2 teaspoon chili powder
1 teaspoon garlic powder
Sea salt and ground black pepper, to taste

Directions

Pat the cauliflower florets dry and reserve.
In a mixing bowl, thoroughly combine the flour, rice milk, chili powder, garlic powder, salt and black pepper.
Dip the cauliflower florets in the batter until well coated on all sides.
Place the cauliflower florets in your freezer for 15 minutes.
Cook the cauliflower in the preheated Air Fryer at 390 degrees F for about 10 minutes; turn them over and cook for another 10 minutes.
Taste, adjust the seasonings and serve warm.

Per serving: 195 Calories; 2.7g Fat; 36g Carbs; 8.1g Protein; 6.5g Sugars

Winter Squash and Tomato Bake

(Ready in about 30 minutes | Servings 4)

Ingredients

Cashew Cream:

1/2 cup sunflower seeds, soaked overnight, rinsed and drained

1/4 cup lime juice

Sea salt, to taste

2 teaspoons nutritional yeast

1 tablespoon tahini

1/2 cup water

Squash:

1 pound winter squash, peeled and sliced

2 tablespoons olive oil

Sea salt and ground black pepper, to taste

Sauce:

2 tablespoons olive oil

2 ripe tomatoes, crushed

6 ounces spinach, torn into small pieces

2 garlic cloves, minced

1 cup vegetable broth

1/2 teaspoon dried rosemary

1/2 teaspoon dried basil

Directions

Mix the ingredients for the cashew cream in your food processor until creamy and uniform. Reserve.

Place the squash slices in the lightly greased casserole dish. Add the olive oil, salt, and black pepper.

Mix all the ingredients for the sauce. Pour the sauce over the vegetables. Bake in the preheated Air Fryer at 390 degrees F for 15 minutes. Top with the cashew cream and bake an additional 5 minutes or until everything is thoroughly heated.

Transfer to a wire rack to cool slightly before sling and serving

Per serving: 330 Calories; 25.3g Fat; 23.2g Carbs; 8.5g Protein; 3.2g Sugars

---

Baked Banana

(Ready in about 20 minutes | Servings 2)

Ingredients

2 just-ripe bananas
2 teaspoons lime juice
2 tablespoons honey
1/4 teaspoon grated nutmeg
1/2 teaspoon ground cinnamon
A pinch of salt

Directions

Toss the banana with all ingredients until well coated. Transfer your bananas to the parchmentlined cooking basket.

Bake in the preheated Air Fryer at 370 degrees F for 12 minutes, turning them over halfway through the cooking time.

Per serving: 202 Calories; 5.9g Fat; 40.2g Carbs; 1.1g Protein; 29g Sugars

Cinnamon Sugar Tortilla Chips

(Ready in about 20 minutes | Servings 4)

Ingredients

4 (10-inch) flour tortillas
1/4 cup vegan margarine, melted
1 ½ tablespoons ground cinnamon
1/4 cup caster sugar

Directions

Slice each tortilla into eight slices. Brush the tortilla pieces with the melted margarine.
In a mixing bowl, thoroughly combine the cinnamon and sugar. Toss the cinnamon mixture with the tortillas.
Transfer to the cooking basket and cook at 360 degrees F for 8 minutes or until lightly golden. Work in batches.
They will crisp up as they cool. Serve.

Per serving: 270 Calories; 14.1g Fat; 32.7g Carbs; 3.8g Protein; 7.7g Sugars

Dessert

Baked Banana with Chocolate

(Ready in about 15 minutes | Servings 2)

Ingredients

2 bananas, peeled and cut in half lengthwise
1 tablespoon coconut oil, melted
1 tablespoon cocoa powder
1 tablespoon agave syrup

Directions

Bake your bananas in the preheated Air Fryer at 370 degrees F for 12 minutes, turning them over halfway through the cooking time.
In the meantime, microwave the coconut oil for 30 seconds; stir in the cocoa powder and agave syrup.
Serve the baked bananas with a few drizzles of the chocolate glaze.

Per serving: 201 Calories; 7.5g Fat; 36.9g Carbs; 1.7g Protein; 23g Sugars

Banana and Pecan Muffins

(Ready in about 25 minutes | Servings 4)

Ingredients

1 extra-large ripe banana, mashed
1/4 cup coconut oil
1 egg
1/4 cup brown sugar
1/2 teaspoon vanilla essence
1/2 teaspoon ground cinnamon
4 tablespoons pecans, chopped
1/2 cup self-rising flour

Directions

Start by preheating your Air Fryer to 330 degrees F.
In a mixing bowl, combine the banana, coconut oil, egg, brown
sugar, vanilla and cinnamon.
Add in the chopped pecans and flour and stir again to combine well.
Spoon the mixture into a lightly greased muffin tin and transfer to
the Air Fryer cooking basket.
Bake your muffins in the preheated Air Fryer for 15 to 17 minutes or
until a tester comes out dry and clean.
Sprinkle some extra icing sugar over the top of each muffin if
desired. Serve.

**Per serving: 315 Calories; 21.4g Fat; 27.9g Carbs; 4.8g Protein;
11.3g Sugars**

Pecan Fudge Brownies

(Ready in about 30 minutes | Servings 6)

Ingredients

1/2 cup butter, melted
1/2 cup sugar
1 teaspoon vanilla essence
1 egg
1/2 cup flour
1/2 teaspoon baking powder
1/4 cup cocoa powder
1/2 teaspoon ground cinnamon
1/4 teaspoon fine sea salt
1 ounce semisweet chocolate, coarsely chopped
1/4 cup pecans, finely chopped

Directions

Start by preheating your Air Fryer to 350 degrees F. Now, lightly grease six silicone molds.
In a mixing dish, beat the melted butter with the sugar until fluffy. Next, stir in the vanilla and egg and beat again.
After that, add the flour, baking powder, cocoa powder, cinnamon, and salt. Mix until everything is well combined.
Fold in the chocolate and pecans; mix to combine. Bake in the preheated Air Fryer for 20 to 22 minutes.

Per serving: 341 Calories; 23.5g Fat; 31.3g Carbs; 4.2g Protein; 19.2g Sugars

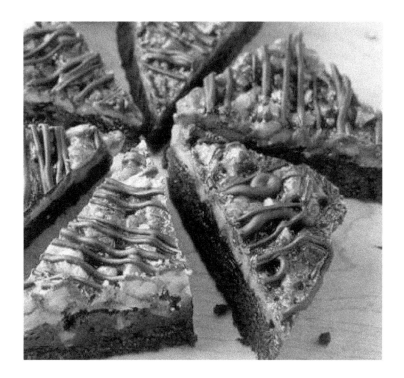

Baked Peaches with Oatmeal Pecan Streusel

(Ready in about 20 minutes | Servings 3)

Ingredients

2 tablespoons old-fashioned rolled oats

3 tablespoons golden caster sugar

1/2 teaspoon ground cinnamon

1 egg

2 tablespoons cold salted butter, cut into pieces

3 tablespoons pecans, chopped

3 large ripe freestone peaches, halved and pitted

Directions

Mix the rolled oats, sugar, cinnamon, egg, and butter until well combined.

Add a big spoonful of prepared topping to the center of each peach.

Pour 1/2 cup of water into an Air Fryer safe dish. Place the peaches in the dish.

Top the peaches with the roughly chopped pecans. Bake at 340 degrees F for 17 minutes. Serve at room temperature.

Per serving: 247 Calories; 14.1g Fat; 28.8g Carbs; 5.9g Protein; 23.1g Sugars

Almond Chocolate Cupcakes

(Ready in about 20 minutes | Servings 6)

Ingredients

3/4 cup self-raising flour
1 cup powdered sugar
1/4 teaspoon salt
1/4 teaspoon nutmeg, preferably freshly grated
1 tablespoon cocoa powder
2 ounces butter, softened
1 egg, whisked
2 tablespoons almond milk
1/2 teaspoon vanilla extract
1 ½ ounces dark chocolate chunks
1/2 cup almonds, chopped

Directions

In a mixing bowl, combine the flour, sugar, salt, nutmeg, and cocoa powder. Mix to combine well.
In another mixing bowl, whisk the butter, egg, almond milk, and vanilla.
Now, add the wet egg mixture to the dry ingredients. Then, carefully fold in the chocolate chunks and almonds; gently stir to combine.
Scrape the batter mixture into muffin cups. Bake your cupcakes at 350 degrees F for 12 minutes until a toothpick comes out clean.
Decorate with chocolate sprinkles if desired. Serve.

Per serving: 288 Calories; 14.7g Fat; 35.1g Carbs; 5.1g Protein; 20g Sugars

Other Air Fryer

Rustic Air Grilled Pears

(Ready in about 10 minutes | Servings 2)

Ingredients

2 pears, cored and halved
2 teaspoons coconut oil, melted
2 teaspoons honey
1/2 teaspoon pure vanilla extract
1/2 teaspoon ground cinnamon
1/4 teaspoon ground cardamom
1 tablespoon rum
2 ounces walnuts

Directions

Drizzle pear halves with the coconut oil and honey.
Sprinkle vanilla, cinnamon, cardamom and rum over your pears. Top them with chopped walnuts.
Air fry your pears at 360 degrees for 8 minutes, checking them halfway through the cooking time.
Drizzle with some extra honey, if desired. Bon appétit!

Per serving: 313 Calories; 23.1g Fat; 22.7g Carbs; 4.7g Protein; 17.5g Sugars

Homemade Party Mix

(Ready in about 10 minutes | Servings 4)

Ingredients

1 cup cheese squares
1 cup Rice Chex
1/2 cup pistachios
1/4 cup sunflower seeds
1/2 cup cheddar-flavored mini pretzel twists
3 tablespoons melted butter
1/2 teaspoon salt
1/4 teaspoon ground black pepper
1/2 teaspoon paprika
1/2 teaspoon shallot powder
1/2 teaspoon porcini powder
1/2 teaspoon garlic powder

Directions

Thoroughly combine all ingredients in a bowl.
Place the mixture in a single layer in the parchment-lined cooking basket.
Bake in the preheated Air Fryer at 330 degrees F for 7 minutes.
Allow the mixture to cool completely.
Bon appétit!

Per serving: 358 Calories; 8.7g Fat; 36.1g Carbs; 21.2g Protein; 2.4g Sugars

Traditional Greek Revithokeftedes

(Ready in about 20 minutes | Servings 4)

Ingredients

2 cups chickpeas, soaked overnight

1 teaspoon fresh garlic, minced

1 red onion, chopped

2 boiled potatoes, peeled and mashed

2 tablespoons all-purpose flour

1 teaspoon Greek spice mix

1 teaspoon olive oil

Directions

In a mixing bowl, thoroughly combine all ingredients until everything is well incorporated. Shape the mixture into equal patties.

Then, transfer the patties to the Air Fryer cooking basket.

Cook the patties at 380 degrees F for about 15 minutes, turning them over halfway through the cooking time.

Serve your revithokeftedes in pita bread with toppings of your choice. Enjoy!

Per serving: 474 Calories; 7.3g Fat; 82g Carbs; 22.4g Protein; 12.5g Sugars

Jamaican Cornmeal Pudding

(Ready in about 1 hour + chilling time | Servings 6)

Ingredients

3 cups coconut milk

2 ounces butter, softened

1 teaspoon cinnamon

1/2 teaspoon grated nutmeg

1 cup sugar

1/2 teaspoon fine sea salt

1 ½ cups yellow cornmeal

1/4 cup all-purpose flour

1/2 cup water

1/2 cup raisins

1 teaspoon rum extract 1 teaspoon vanilla extract Custard:

1/2 cup full-fat coconut milk

1 ounce butter

1/4 cup honey

1 dash vanilla

Directions

Place the coconut milk, butter, cinnamon, nutmeg, sugar, and salt in a large saucepan; bring to a rapid boil. Heat off.

In a mixing bowl, thoroughly combine the cornmeal, flour and water; mix to combine well.

Add the milk/butter mixture to the cornmeal mixture; mix to combine. Bring the cornmeal mixture to boil; then, reduce the heat and simmer approximately 7 minutes, whisking continuously.

Remove from the heat. Now, add the raisins, rum extract, and vanilla. Place the mixture into a lightly greased baking pan and bake at 325 degrees F for 12 minutes.

In a saucepan, whisk the coconut milk, butter, honey, and vanilla; let it simmer for 2 to 3 minutes. Now, prick your pudding with a fork and top with the prepared custard.

Return to your Air Fryer and bake for about 35 minutes more or until a toothpick inserted comes out dry and clean. Place in your refrigerator until ready to serve. Bon appétit!

Per serving: 538 Calories; 21.5g Fat; 82.4g Carbs; 8.2g Protein; 49.4g Sugars

Baked Eggs with Kale and Ham

(Ready in about 15 minutes | Servings 2)

Ingredients

2 eggs
1/4 teaspoon dried or fresh marjoram
2 teaspoons chili powder
1/3 teaspoon kosher salt
½ cup steamed kale
1/4 teaspoon dried or fresh rosemary
4 pork ham slices
1/3 teaspoon ground black pepper, or more to taste

Directions

Divide the kale and ham among 2 ramekins; crack an egg into each ramekin. Sprinkle with seasonings.
Cook for 15 minutes at 335 degrees F or until your eggs reach desired texture.
Serve warm with spicy tomato ketchup and pickles. Bon appétit!

Per serving: 417 Calories; 17.8g Fat; 3g Carbs; 61g Protein; 0.9g Sugars

Old-Fashioned Beef Stroganoff

(Ready in about 20 minutes | Servings 4)

Ingredients

3/4 pound beef sirloin steak, cut into small-sized strips
1/4 cup balsamic vinegar
1 tablespoon brown mustard
2 tablespoons all-purpose flour
1 tablespoon butter
1 cup beef broth
1 cup leek, chopped
2 cloves garlic, crushed
1 teaspoon cayenne pepper
Sea salt flakes and crushed red pepper, to taste
1 cup sour cream
2 ½ tablespoons tomato paste

Directions

Place the beef along with the balsamic vinegar and the mustard in a mixing dish; cover and marinate in your refrigerator for about 1 hour.
Then, coat the beef strips with the flour; butter the inside of a baking dish and put the beef into the dish.
Add the broth, leeks and garlic. Cook at 380 degrees for 8 minutes.
Pause the machine and add the cayenne pepper, salt, red pepper, sour cream and tomato paste; cook for additional 7 minutes.
Check for doneness and serve with warm egg noodles, if desired.
Bon appétit!

Per serving: 352 Calories; 20.8g Fat; 10.0g Carbs; 29.8g Protein; 1.4g Sugars

Chicken Drumsticks with Ketchup-Lemon Sauce

(Ready in about 20 minutes + marinating time | Servings 6)

Ingredients

3 tablespoons lemon juice
1 cup tomato ketchup
1 ½ tablespoons fresh rosemary, chopped
6 skin-on chicken drumsticks, boneless
1/2 teaspoon ground black pepper
2 teaspoons lemon zest, grated
1/3 cup honey
3 cloves garlic, minced

Directions

Dump the chicken drumsticks into a mixing dish. Now, add the other items and give it a good stir; let it marinate overnight in your refrigerator.
Discard the marinade; roast the chicken legs in your air fryer at 375 degrees F for 22 minutes, turning once.
Now, add the marinade and cook an additional 6 minutes or until everything is warmed through.

Per serving: 274 Calories; 12g Fat; 17.3g Carbs; 23.3g Protein; 16.2g Sugars

Creamy Lemon Turkey

(Ready in about 2 hours 25 minutes | Servings 4)

Ingredients

1/3 cup sour cream
1 cloves garlic, finely minced
1/3 teaspoon lemon zest
2 small-sized turkey breasts, skinless and cubed
1/3 cup thickened cream
2 tablespoons lemon juice
1 teaspoon fresh marjoram, chopped
Salt and freshly cracked mixed peppercorns, to taste
1/2 cup scallion, chopped
1/2 can tomatoes, diced
1 ½ tablespoons canola oil

Directions

Firstly, pat dry the turkey breast. Mix the remaining items; marinate the turkey for 2 hours.
Set the air fryer to cook at 355 degrees F. Brush the turkey with a nonstick spray; cook for 23 minutes, turning once. Serve with naan and enjoy!

Per serving: 260 Calories; 15.3g Fat; 8.9g Carbs; 28.6g Protein; 1.9g Sugars

The Best Sweet Potato Fries Ever

(Ready in about 20 minutes | Servings 4)

Ingredients

1 1/2 tablespoons olive oil
1/2 teaspoon smoked cayenne pepper
3 sweet potatoes, peeled and cut into 1/4-inch long slices
1/2 teaspoon shallot powder
1/3 teaspoon freshly ground black pepper, or more to taste
3/4 teaspoon garlic salt

Directions

Firstly, preheat your air fryer to 360 degrees F.
Then, add the sweet potatoes to a mixing dish; toss them with the other ingredients.
Cook the sweet potatoes approximately 14 minutes. Serve with a dipping sauce of choice.

Per serving: 180 Calories; 5.4g Fat; 31.8g Carbs; 1.8g Protein; 0.7g Sugars

CPSIA information can be obtained
at www.ICGtesting.com
Printed in the USA
LVHW080333070621
689542LV00002B/33